Quilt National
2005

Quilt National
2005

Coproduced by
Lark Books &
the Dairy Barn Cultural Arts Center

LARK BOOKS
A Division of Sterling Publishing Co., Inc.
New York

Quilt National Project Director: **Hilary Morrow Fletcher**
Editor: **Susan Mowery Kieffer**
Art Director: **Kathleen Holmes**
Photographer: **Brian Blauser**
Cover Designer: **Barbara Zaretsky**
Editorial Assistance: **Delores Gosnell, Rebecca Guthrie**
Editorial Intern: **Megan S. McCarter**
Art Assistance: **Brad Armstrong, Chris Dollar**
Additional photography: **Bob Barrett** (page 9), **David Belda**
(page 10), **David Caras** (page 13), **Gerhard**
Heidersberger (page 23), **Joe Ofria/Image Inn** (page 32),
James Dewrance (page 33), **Gerhard Heidersberger**
(page 35), **Karen Bell** (page 59), **Richard Johns** (page 61),
Bronz Photography (page 69), **Karen Bell** (page 76),
Michael Wicks (page 77), **William Taylor** (page 92), **David**
Caras (page 95), **Karen Bell** (page 97), **Luke Jordan** (page
103), **Doug Van der Zande** (page 180)

Library of Congress Cataloging-in-Publication Data

Quilt National (2005 : Athens, Ohio)
    Quilt national 2005 : the best of contemporary quilts / by Susan Mowery
Kieffer ; Coproduced by Lark Books & the Dairy Barn Cultural Arts Center.—1st ed.
        p.   cm.
    Includes index.
    ISBN 1-57990-677-X (hardcover)
    1. Art quilts—United States—History—21st century—Exhibitions. 2. Art quilts—
History—21st century—Exhibitions. I. Kieffer, Susan Mowery. II. Dairy Barn South-
eastern Ohio Cultural Arts Center. III. Title.
    NK9112.Q5 2005
    746.46'0973'07477197—dc22
                            2004027582

10 9 8 7 6 5 4 3 2 1

First Edition

Published by Lark Books, A Division of Sterling Publishing Co., Inc.
387 Park Avenue South, New York, N.Y. 10016

© 2005, Lark Books

Distributed in Canada by Sterling Publishing, c/o Canadian Manda Group,
165 Dufferin Street, Toronto, Ontario, Canada M6K 3H6

Distributed in the U.K. by Guild of Master Craftsman Publications Ltd., Castle Place,
166 High Street, Lewes, East Sussex, England BN7 1XU Tel: (+ 44) 1273 477374,
Fax: (+ 44) 1273 478606, e-mail: pubs@thegmcgroup.com,
Web: www.gmcpublications.com

Distributed in Australia by Capricorn Link (Australia) Pty Ltd., P.O. Box 704, Windsor,
NSW 2756 Australia

If you have questions or comments about this book, please contact:

Lark Books
67 Broadway
Asheville, NC 28801
(828) 253-0467

Manufactured in China

ISBN 1-57990-677-X

For information about custom editions, special sales, premium and corporate
purchases, please contact Sterling Special Sales Department at 800-805-5489
or special sales@sterlingpub.com.

Cover: Jeanne Williamson

Front flap: Jean Cacicedo

Title page: Harumi Iida

Opposite page, top to bottom: Joy Saville,
Mary Anne Jordan, Jane A. Sassaman

Page 6, top to bottom: Sue Pierce,
Emily Richardson, Janet Steadman

Page 7, top to bottom: Lori Lupe Pelish,
Sue Benner, Anna Torma

Page 8, top to bottom: Linda Levin, Lisa Call,
Barbara J. Schneider

Back flap: Lisa Call

Back cover: Linda Colsh
Mary Anne Jordan

Contents

Foreword

A QUILT MASTERPIECE is always more than the sum of its parts. Each unit plays such a critical role that the quality of the finished object would be significantly compromised if it were not there.

This is the 14th biennial, international juried exhibition, intended to showcase the breadth and depth of talent of fiber artists from around the world. The works are by more than 80 artists from 27 states and seven foreign countries.

On behalf of the board of trustees of the Dairy Barn Cultural Arts Center, I would like to take this opportunity to acknowledge and express our most heartfelt gratitude to the businesses, organizations, and individuals whose generosity and efforts make it possible for us, once again, to present the work of some of the most talented artists working in the medium today.

As a very small, non-profit organization, the Dairy Barn Cultural Arts Center is dependent on the continued support of our sponsors whose names are listed below. Quilt National would be impossible without their vital assistance.

This beautiful book enables those who visit the exhibition to remember what they saw and others to appreciate what they missed. Our thanks go to the personnel at Lark Books, including Carol Taylor, President and Publisher; Editor Susan Mowery Kieffer; and Art Director Kathleen J. Holmes.

Thanks also to jurors Mark Richard Leach, M. Joan Lintault, and Miriam Nathan-Roberts for their thoughtful decisions in assembling the works in this exhibition.

We are also grateful to the hundreds of artists from more than 20 countries who felt Quilt National was worthy of their efforts.

Lastly, we want to recognize the unceasing energy and commitment to Quilt National and to the Dairy Barn by exhibition designer and volunteer extraordinaire Sarah Williams, photographer Brian Blauser, the members of the Dairy Barn staff, and the dozens of members of the Athens, Ohio, community whose efforts make it possible for Project Director Hilary Fletcher to stitch together the masterpiece that is Quilt National.

I know the other members of the board of trustees join me in inviting you to make frequent visits to the Dairy Barn Cultural Arts Center. Our year-round program of exhibitions and events and our exciting Gallery Shop will make your visit more than worthwhile.

Elizabethe Riggs Kramer, President
Board of Trustees
Dairy Barn Cultural Arts Center

Major support is provided by:
> **Fairfield Processing Corporation, maker of Poly-fil brand fiber products**
> **Husqvarna Viking**
> ***Quilts Japan* Magazine/Nihon Vogue Co., Ltd.**

Additional support comes from the following businesses and organizations:
> **Amerihost of Athens**
> **Athens Convention and Visitors Bureau**
> **FreeSpirit Fabrics**
> **Friends of Fiber Art International**
> **The James Foundation**
> **Ohio Arts Council**
> **Ohio Quilts!!**
> **Studio Art Quilt Associates**

And the following generous individuals:
> **Joe and Lynda Berman**
> **Warren and Nancy Brakensiek**
> **Nancy Erickson**
> **Betty Goodwin**
> **The McCarthy family**

Introduction

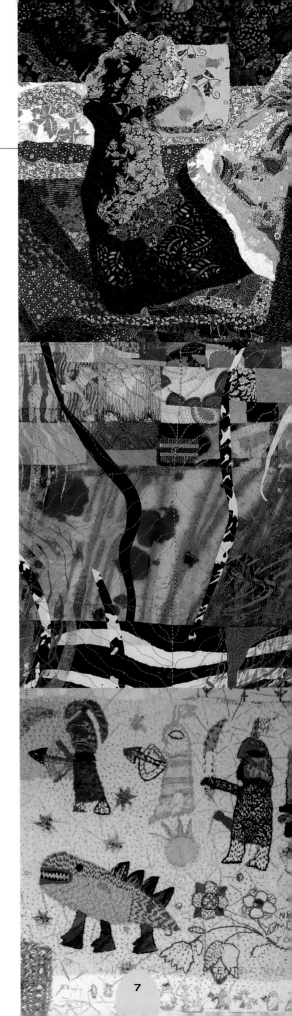

PERHAPS IT'S BECAUSE I'm getting older that I find myself casting green eyes on my already-retired friends. They have time to travel, to pursue lifelong interests, and to develop new ones. I look at my ever-increasing fabric stash and wonder if I'm likely to make a dent in it. (If not, it will become a legacy for my granddaughter who, with my help, made her first quilt at age four.) Although I'm not quite ready to leave the Dairy Barn and Quilt National (I'll need another two years to sort through the papers and memorabilia that have been accumulating in my office), I'm certainly nearing the end of my tenure.

When I consider my 22 years as Quilt National Project Director, the title of Irving Stone's novel comes to mind—*The Agony and the Ecstasy.*

I experience moments of agony when I ponder the pool of potential jurors who might accept the awesome responsibility of viewing many hundreds of entry slides and selecting the works for a show. Do they have enough name recognition so that established artists will feel they're qualified to evaluate what's presented to them? Will the three people, who may be meeting for the first time, gel into a cohesive group, despite differing tastes and familiarity with the medium? How many of my personal favorites will they select? (My record is about 25 percent.)

There are more moments of agony as I compose the *letter.* How do I tell people that their work wasn't chosen and, at the same time, let them know that their efforts were appreciated, and give them hope and encouragement in the face of disappointment? I'm mindful that, while many understand that getting a *we're sorry* letter goes with the territory when you enter competitions, others may still feel tentative about their work, and their self-confidence might be easily shaken.

The final moments of agony come when the exhibition and/or tour ends and I say a final good-bye to objects that I've come to love. They've given me such pleasure, and I know that I'm unlikely to see them again.

As difficult as these moments are, they are fortunately few and fleeting when compared with the countless hours of ecstasy, joy, satisfaction, and optimism.

I love the pleasure of discovery as I study the similarities and differences among the pieces. Many of the works in this collection reflect an interest in food: fruits, vegetables, and whole grain breads—the foundation blocks of good nutrition. Other works invite us to feast on sustenance for the spirit: personal and family histories, the beauty of plants, bodies of water, and the sunsets that enhance our natural environment, the simplicity of pattern in man-made objects, and the subtle and wonderful interactions of color, texture, and line in abstract images. Just as I encourage visitors to look at the exhibition, and to return again after lunch or on another day, I hope that the readers of this book will visit the works again and again. There is so much to see. I can almost guarantee that with each visit there will be new insights and discoveries. There has seldom been a time when, after countless visits to an exhibition, my husband has not said, "I never saw that one before; you must have just put it up."

As wonderful as it is to get to know the quilts, getting to know the quilt makers is even better. Almost without exception, the artists have been friendly, cooperative, and grateful for my efforts to promote an appreciation of all kinds of quilts. With each Quilt National opening, I have the

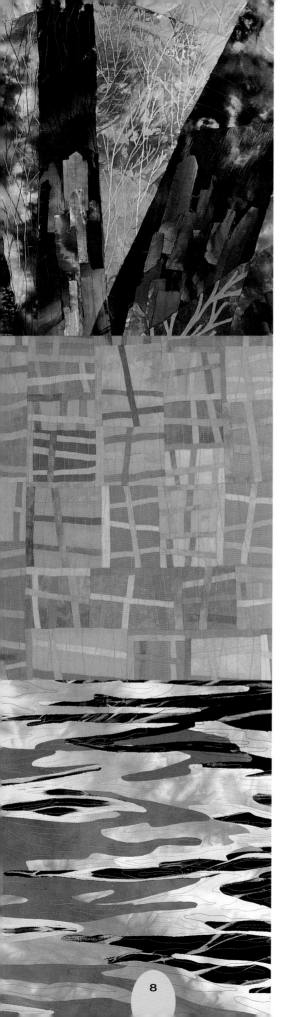

opportunity to make new friends and catch up on family news of others since our last meeting two or more years earlier.

I feel immense joy in being surrounded by the quilts in my home. I love being a collector and being able to rotate these quilts so that I can rediscover their unique elements when, after perhaps several years' absence, they are once again where I can see them every day. I love knowing, too, that I'm not alone in my desire to live with quilts. With each Quilt National, there are more quilts sold, and more collectors who buy multiple works. I strongly agree with the motto of Friends of Fiber Art International: "The best gift one can give a fiber artist is a fiber collector."

Nothing compares, however, to the ecstasy of a zealot who succeeds in drawing more people into the fold. That's what I feel when I learn that a first-time exhibitor began making art quilts after seeing an earlier QN catalog or exhibition. I feel elated when a first-time visitor reluctantly walks into an exhibition—although they have absolutely no interest in quilts—and later announces, "We'll see you again in two years." I take great pleasure when my eye doctor, after having me as a patient for six years, says that he and his family visited a quilt museum while they were on vacation.

Yes, some visitors still expect to see bed-sized works with familiar designs, but there are fewer now than when Quilt National began. And even after nearly 30 years, when I visit quilt shops in all parts of the country, the words Quilt National elicit only the faintest (and often inaccurate) recognition—"Oh, you mean the show in Paducah?"

Despite the fact that those who make and appreciate quilted wall hangings are a very small and largely invisible minority of the quilting world, I see a bright future for the art quilt. More than a third of the entrants for this competition were newbies who had never entered a previous QN. More than 40 percent of the works are by first-time exhibitors, although not necessarily first-time entrants. Persistence can pay off. Works that meet the standards of a competition such as this one have been produced, most likely, by serious artists who make the effort to educate themselves through workshops and independent study. Their works speak with a clear and unique voice. It is they who will ensure the future of the art form.

Increasingly, there are more people who make a conscious effort to visit Quilt National here at the Dairy Barn and at the host venues. A majority of the Dairy Barn visitors travel more than 100 miles to get here. I feel exhilaration when a host venue books another QN collection because their visitors want to see more.

I admit to feeling despair (and perhaps some agony) when I think of the countless masterpieces that have been lost because their makers didn't consider themselves to be artists, and the world failed to recognize the importance of objects that had aesthetic strength as well as function. While it's impossible to reclaim heritage pieces, there are more collectors and institutions today than ever before that accept a responsibility to protect some of today's masterpieces so that future generations can admire and be inspired by them.

I believe with all my heart that the quilt as an art form will not only survive, but it will thrive, and that more and more of these amazing objects will find their way into the mainstream of contemporary art. That is cause for the ultimate ecstasy.

Hilary Morrow Fletcher
Quilt National Project Director

M. Joan Lintault

Quilt National is the exhibition by which all other quilt exhibitions are judged. When I was chosen to be on this jury, I felt honored. Being a member of a jury that puts together an exhibition by choosing the most innovative, visually stimulating, and contemporary quilts from more than 1,200 quilts entered was a great responsibility. Our viewing of the slides was made easier because of the care, organization, and thoroughness of Hilary Fletcher and her team of excellent volunteers. The way they assembled and presented the slides made this overwhelming job a bit easier.

My personal responsibility and goal was to select quilts in which the media and manner of working would be relevant in this new century. I always want to see creativity, critical thinking, and visual expression in the use of fabric, subject matter, and content. What I did not want to see were memes.

A meme is a contagious idea that replicates itself like a virus and is passed from mind to mind. An idea or information pattern is not a meme until it causes someone to replicate it, to repeat it

to someone else, and then another, until it is forever folding in on itself. If working with constructed textiles as quilts is to be considered art, then the constant replication of the same themes, construction techniques, and reworked ideas should not be part of this exhibition.

The quilts chosen are extremely varied—from traditional to conceptual. The fabrics chosen were commercial to hand-dyed. The techniques are diverse—from embroidery to gestural marks on fabric. I believe they show the range of possibilities of working with fabric. Technique, craftsmanship, or subject alone does not make a successful work; infusing the work with the artist's personality and individual touch is what makes the work provocative.

Entering the competition is an act of emotional courage. I recognize the risk of rejection everyone must face. The slides were anonymous to us. Looking at them was quite poignant when we realized the time, love, and energy that went into each piece. Everyone who entered is encouraged to continue working and entering their best work in future competitions. I am very grateful for everyone's participation in this exhibition. I realize that most of us have to fit our artwork into busy lives. Every minute we can work is a gift.

M. Joan Lintault
New Paltz, New York

Fan Dancer

Invitational Work: Quilt National 2005 Juror
Cotton, sequins, beads; painted, hand dyed, screenprinted, appliquéd, machine quilted; 56 x 59 inches (142 x 150 cm)

This piece is one in a new series of quilts. I have always been interested in using the idea of portraits and the expressive use of visual form to tell a story.

Miriam Nathan-Roberts

I have been entering Quilt National since 1982 and know full well how it feels to receive both a letter of acceptance and one of non-acceptance. When I was asked to jury the 2005 QN, I did not expect those feelings to wash over me during the process, but they did. After seeing the entire set of slides the first night, I was overwhelmed by the sheer number of hours the work represented and the hopes and trepidations those slides represented.

In the months before the judging, thinking about what was important to me in art quilts became a preoccupation. Going to Athens, Ohio, I was sure that I would judge purely on good composition, design, and visual impact. I believe that the artist's concept and vision should dictate all the aspects of the work. The design, materials chosen, and techniques should all support that concept. This was all well

Miriam Nathan-Roberts

Berkeley, California

Japan, April 2003
Invitational Work:
Quilt National 2005 Juror

Whole-cloth silk crêpe de Chine, digitally manipulated image; digitally printed, machine quilted; 64 x 50 inches (163 x 127 cm)

For the last few years, I have been marrying digital art and printing with stitched and quilted textiles. In this piece my goal was to focus on the beauty of everyday life. In Japan, even in the humblest of places, I have seen stunning patterns in the arrangement of the most ordinary items. By enlarging and manipulating my photograph, I use the power of scale to call attention to the essence of the image. This quilt is typical of my recent work.

and good in theory, but, in fact, you cannot divorce the medium, in this case primarily fabric, from the work. There are things that can be done in paint or other media that are extremely difficult to do in fabric.

Of course, in any competition of this type, the quality of the slide is very important. I cannot stress that enough! In going through such a large number of slides, the amount of time any one slide is seen makes that image quality of vital importance. It would truly be lovely to have the luxury of judging from the pieces themselves but I, myself, don't enter shows that have that requirement.

Narrowing down 1,200 entries to 80 pieces is a formidable task, given that the entries are already self-selected by the artists who feel they are doing work that is worthy of the reputation of Quilt National. This task was made so much easier by the organization of Hilary Fletcher and her committed staff of volunteers. Indeed, without their work, our job would have been almost impossible.

The quality of the work was very good. I think that no matter who had been on the jury, the final 200 to 300 pieces would have been the ones chosen. At this point, the choices become very difficult and are determined by what the individual jurors bring to the table. There were some quilts of extraordinary workmanship and beauty but whose images were overused. The quilts that were chosen had something intriguing or unique about them that compelled us to want to see them again.

The quilt by Jean Cacicedo, *Markers: Style 2-504,* brought a new approach to quilt making. The reference to textiles in their most common use—the making of clothing—was executed in materials and techniques unusual in the art quilt world. The image is strong, clear, and unique, as well as being beautifully executed.

I chose Clare Plug's quilt *To R.H. 2* for my Juror's Award for several reasons. The image is striking and self-referential to quilts. Using a faux comforter as the image was a nice bit of tongue-in-cheek and pleased my sense of fun. The control of the discharge process and the workmanship is very impressive.

The changes in both The Dairy Barn and the quilts in Quilt National since my first visit in 1983 have been great and all for the better. I wonder what the next 22 years will bring.

Jurors' Bios - Quilt National 05

Mark Richard Leach

Mark Richard Leach is founding director of the Mint Museum of Craft + Design in Charlotte, North Carolina. He currently holds the post of Deputy Director of the Mint Museums, which include the Mint Museum of Craft + Design, and the Mint Museum of Art. He has held curatorial posts in several states and has taught, lectured, and moderated panels on public and environmental art, art criticism, and curatorship. He has published numerous texts on art, and has authored articles for such publications as the *Journal of Arts Management, Law, & Society, New Art Examiner, Metalsmith, Artvu, FIBERARTS,* and *American Ceramics.* He is a trustee of the Art Alliance for Contemporary Glass and a former trustee of the American Craft Council, where he served on the council's executive committee as chair of the publishing committee, overseeing *American Craft* Magazine.

M. Joan Lintault

M. Joan Lintault lives and works in New York State. She is an internationally renowned quilter who is among a handful of the original art quilters. She has been involved in the fibers movement and has been exhibiting her work since 1965. In his book *The Art Quilt,* Robert Shaw called her "...one of the most consistent and original of all contemporary quilt makers." She has studied, taught, and lectured on various surface design techniques in the United States, India, China, Malaysia, and Japan. Her work has been exhibited at the Illinois State Museum, the Renwick Gallery at the Smithsonian American Art Museum, the American Craft Museum, and the American Museum of Quilts and Textiles. She has shown her work in more than 275 exhibitions. Ms. Lintault's work can be found in both public and private collections.

Miriam Nathan-Roberts

Miriam Nathan-Roberts has been making quilts since the early 1970s. After studying textiles and design at Cornell University, she pursued a master's degree at the University of California at Berkeley. Subsequently, she taught in public schools for nearly 30 years. As she rode home from the hospital after the birth of her son, she stopped to buy fabric for *Kyoto,* which became the first of nine quilts she has exhibited at Quilt National. One of her QN works was granted a Best of Show Award, and another was the recipient of a People's Choice Award. Since then, Miriam's quilts have toured throughout the United States, Europe, and Japan. Her quilt *Changing Planes* was selected as one of 100 "Best American Quilts of the Twentieth Century," an historic 1999 show in Houston, Texas. She continues to travel, lecturing and teaching workshops on art-quilt design. She resides in Berkeley, California.

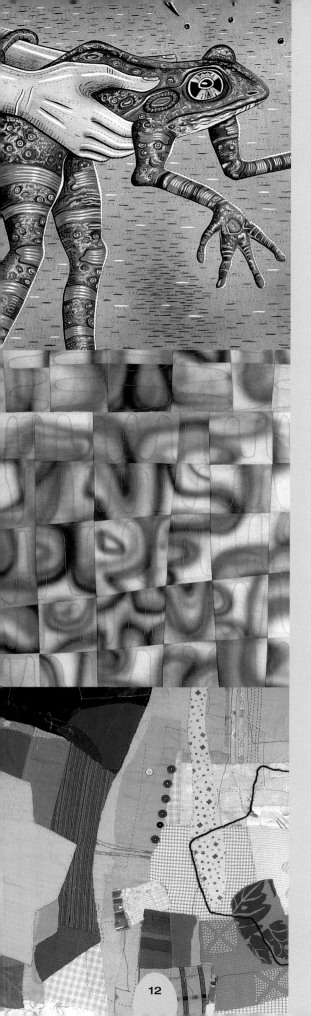

the Quilts

From top to bottom: **Linda MacDonald,**
Sandy Shelenberger, Anne Smith

12

Jeanne Williamson
Natick, Massachusetts

Orange Construction Fence Series #29

Cotton; monoprinted, hand stamped on front and back, machine quilted; 38 x 46 inches (97 x 117 cm)

I combined the grids of three construction fences when I printed the fabric for *Orange Construction Fence Series #29*. I wanted to show the difference in grid patterns and how we can see the sky and grass through the holes. After this piece was quilted, I painted the blues of the sky and the greens of the grass on the back so they would bleed through the front to create a softer look.

Janet Steadman

Clinton, Washington

Western Exposure

Cotton hand dyed by the artist;
machine pieced and quilted;
53 x 41 inches (135 x 104 cm)

My Whidbey Island home on the shores of Useless Bay faces west. Intense fiery sunsets fill our huge western windows with glorious color. In my workspace, I turn my back on the distractions of the natural beauty visible from my beachfront windows and in doing so, I invent for myself a new aesthetic space where I can create unique visions of nature's beauty, visions like watching sunsets through windows with a western exposure.

Marla Hattabaugh

Scottsdale, Arizona

So Cal Pals

Cotton; machine pieced,
hand quilted; 83 x 84 inches
(211 x 213 cm)

Making quilts is my passion
and joy. It's a way of life
that brings me friends, fun,
learning, and traveling.

Mirjam Pet-Jacobs

Waalre, The Netherlands

Mimiquilt IX: Solidarity

Silk and cotton-blend fabrics
hand painted and dyed by the
artist; stamped, machine
pieced, hand appliquéd, hand
and machine quilted; 52 x 56
inches (132 x 142 cm)

Mimis are long, thin spirits who, in ancient times, taught the Australian Aboriginals all they needed to know to survive. Inspired by the so-called hollow-log *mimis* from Arnhemland, Australia, I designed a specific *mimi*-shape to show several aspects of human life. This quilt deals with the fact that in times of trouble, people help one another. A neighbor across from me experienced this when her husband fell ill and died from cancer.

Linda Colsh

Everberg, Belgium

Lost Rites

Cotton, silk; dyed and screen-printed by the artist, machine pieced and quilted; 42 x 51 inches (107 x 130 cm)

Myth and ritual have meanings that evolve across time. Some things become bigger than life, and others, in whole or part, are lost. We tend to look back at earlier civilizations through filters set up by our own civilization. I prefer to cast a wider net and consider other possibilities.

Sandy Shelenberger

Conneaut, Ohio

Black & Blue #3: Process

Cotton, textile paint; airbrushed by the
artist, machine pieced and quilted;
36 x 53 inches (91 x 135 cm)

Black & Blue #3: Process is part of a series of personal messages that explores letting go while wanting to hang on. The work changes and evolves as the resistance fades. Pieces/parts of letters show, like a puzzle to be solved. *Process* is a positive message about working through life's issues.

Emily Richardson

Philadelphia, Pennsylvania

Water Glass

Silk, acrylic paint, cotton embroidery thread; hand stitched,
embroidered, and quilted;
21 x 28 inches (71 x 53 cm)

My attraction to working in fiber stems from the range of possibilities offered by the materials and techniques. From the fluid act of painting on cloth, to the focused visual attention of arranging parts, to the tactile working of the stitches, I am continually excited by what I see. *Water Glass* offers a view similar to objects seen through water. Shifts of light and position, and interruptions of the surface change the appearance of what is below. Movement, bending, and uncertain placement are suggested.

Pamela Grammer
Charlottesville, Virginia

I Remember in My Back
Cotton broadcloth hand dyed by the artist, nylon fabric, fabric paint; machine and hand appliquéd, machine quilted; 56 x 34 inches (142 x 86 cm)

Many people believe that the memory of trauma is stored not only in the brain, but in the cells of the body. This piece is about the process of coming to a place of peace with that trauma, but not forgetting the memories, because that is likely impossible. *I Remember in My Back* is one in a group of eleven pieces about the mental and physical challenges people live with and the process of healing.

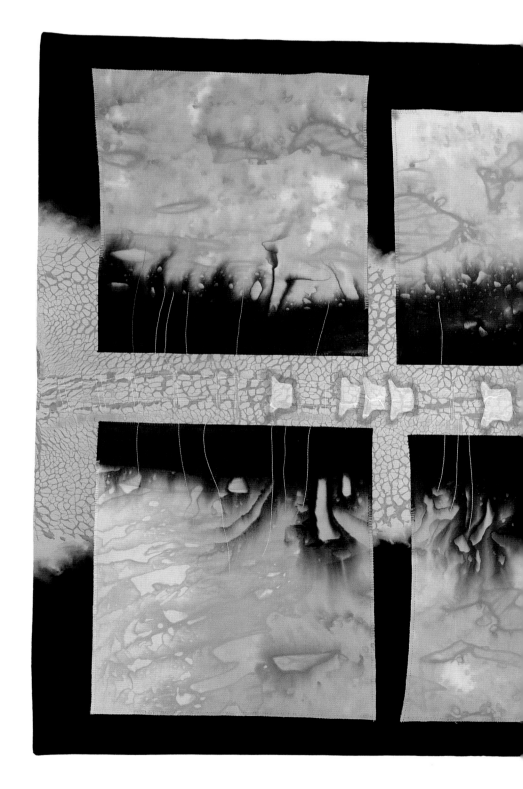

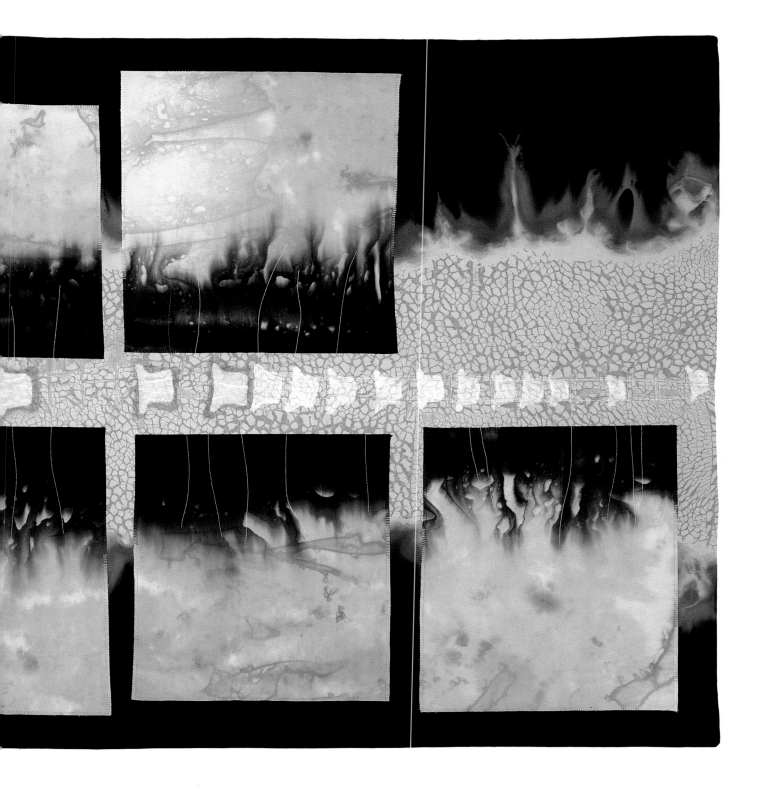

Bob Adams

Lafayette, Indiana

Lunar No. 6 Harvest Moons

Cotton; discharged, pieced, raw-edge appliquéd, machine sewn; 54 x 40 inches (137 x 102 cm)

I have been working for a few years on my "Lunar" series. *Harvest Moons* evolved during the fall when the farmers were harvesting their crops and mother nature was painting the landscape with earthy colors. I used black cloth that discharged to earthy browns. The moons reflect the season, as do the other shapes incorporated into the piece.

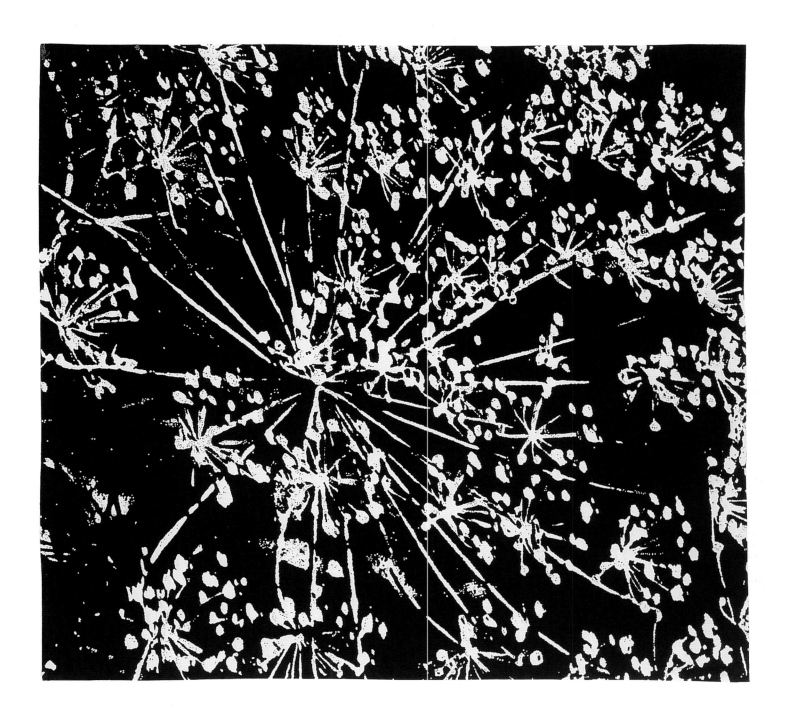

Barbara W. Watler
Hollywood, Florida

Ebullient Efflorescence

Cotton, batting, muslin backing;
hand basted, machine satin
stitched, reverse appliquéd;
61 x 57 inches (155 x 145 cm)

This small sprig of fennel is magnified to enhance the explosive magnificence of the bloom. The fractal-like images suggest movement and evolution from the small bits to the whole bloom.

Eliza Brewster

Honesdale, Pennsylvania

And Then They Came For Me

Commercial fabric, photo transfer,
permanent markers, ink; color discharged, hand appliquéd and quilted;
38 x 23 inches (97 x 58 cm)

I work in an improvisational way in the
sense that I have the germ of an idea, a
visual snapshot if you will, that then
develops over many weeks. In this
case, someone gave me a pin with the
quote of the title and, coupled with what
I see as the rise of anti-Semitism, I was
motivated to make this quilt.

Linda Kyle Campbell

Lawrenceville, Georgia

Tracks on Stone

Hand-dyed cotton, acrylic paint, dye; screenprinted, shibori resist, painted, discharged, machine pieced and quilted; 42 x 59 inches (107 x 150 cm)

This piece is a memorial to my father-in-law and was inspired by a photograph of him as a young man in the 1930s. The genesis came about when my husband inherited some boxes of photographs no one in the family had seen before. I felt an urge to capture this one image and explore memories and stories that may or may not get passed down. It's about a family legacy that will end with the current generation.

Dinah Sargeant

Newhall, California

Mandalas

Cotton fabric hand painted by the artist;
machine pieced, hand and machine appliquéd,
hand embroidered, hand and machine quilted;
67 x 54 inches (170 x 137 cm)

Coins and torn leaves;

A mandala was left at the foot of the bed,

Spurred by some primitive memory,

Lovingly arranged by our three-year-old daughter,

For a quiet discovery.

Robert S. Leathers
Jamul, California

Heullas (Tracks)
Cotton (hand dyed by Judy Robertson), inkjet photo transfer, found objects; machine pieced, appliquéd, and quilted; 66 x 41 inches (168 x 104 cm)

Tracks refers to footprints left by illegals from Mexico. While hiking near my home I found five blanket pieces. These *carpet booties*, as they are called by the border patrol, had been tied by illegals around their shoes to cover their tracks and then discarded when they were transported by *coyotes*. It is a perilous journey from their roots in poor countries to their vision of an American dream. The desperateness of that journey seems to emanate from the tattered cloth.

Barbara Frey
Boulder, Colorado

Night Shift on Mt. Wilson
Cotton (some dye painted by the artist); machine and hand embroidered, machine pieced and quilted; 36 x 36 inches (91 x 91 cm)

I love to put things together to see what they look like. I love colors. I love the feel, the look, the texture, the pattern, and the language of fabric. When my son began fighting wild-land fires, I poured my creative energies into a series of fire quilts. This piece is a dance between his adventurous nature and my maternal instincts, between fire and vulnerability, between nature's beauty and nature's awesome power.

Georgie Cline
Columbus, Ohio

The Whole – Orange Flowers
Commercial and hand-dyed cotton,
netting; fused, collaged, direct
appliquéd, hand and machine quilted;
36 x 36 inches (91 x 91 cm)

I look at nature in several ways—the whole, in fragments, and in bits and pieces. This piece is the whole, trying to create a watercolor painting or a photograph. The images are from a photograph taken at the Frankfurt Botanical Garden in Germany. I started with a single piece of fabric, layering small pieces of fabric, then larger ones, to create depth and space.

Linda Levin
Wayland, Massachusetts

Central Park West Night III
Cotton hand dyed by the
artist, sheer fabric; hand and
machine appliquéd, machine
embroidered and quilted;
64 x 51 inches (163 x 130 cm)

This quilt was made with fabric that I dyed and then constructed in a collage-like manner with sheer overlays and stitching to embellish it. I tried to capture the overall impression of the park, surrounded by tall buildings, and the exciting juxtaposition the location creates.

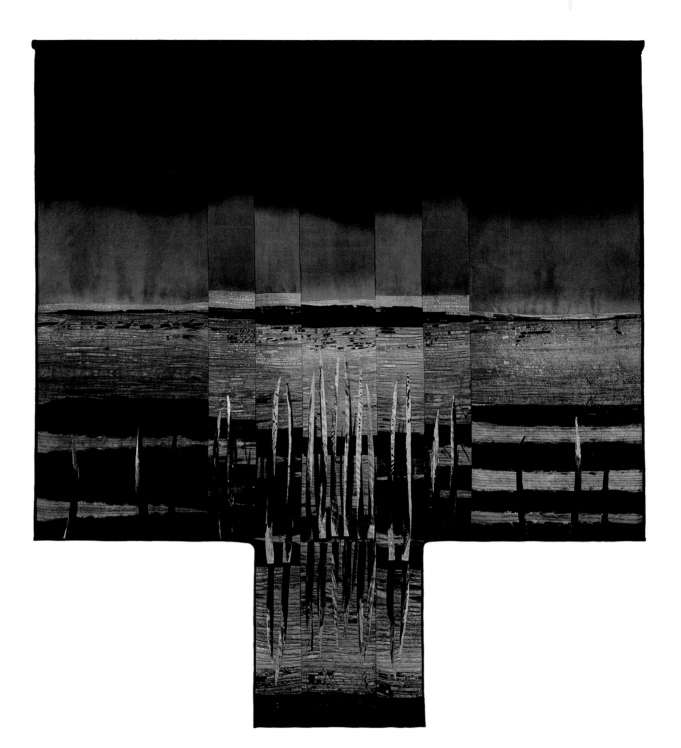

Judith Content
Palo Alto, California

La Brière
Black Thai silk; discharged, shibori dyed, pieced, painted, machine quilted and hand appliquéd; 57 x 66 inches (145 x 168 cm)

The Loire River travels more than a thousand kilometers across France before it enters the Atlantic Ocean at the base of the peninsula of Brittany. Here, I visited Parc Naturel Regional de Brière, a vast salt marsh, hauntingly beautiful and virtually impenetrable. Fortunately, isolation from the outside world protected La Brière until its importance as a marine sanctuary was recognized and preserved.

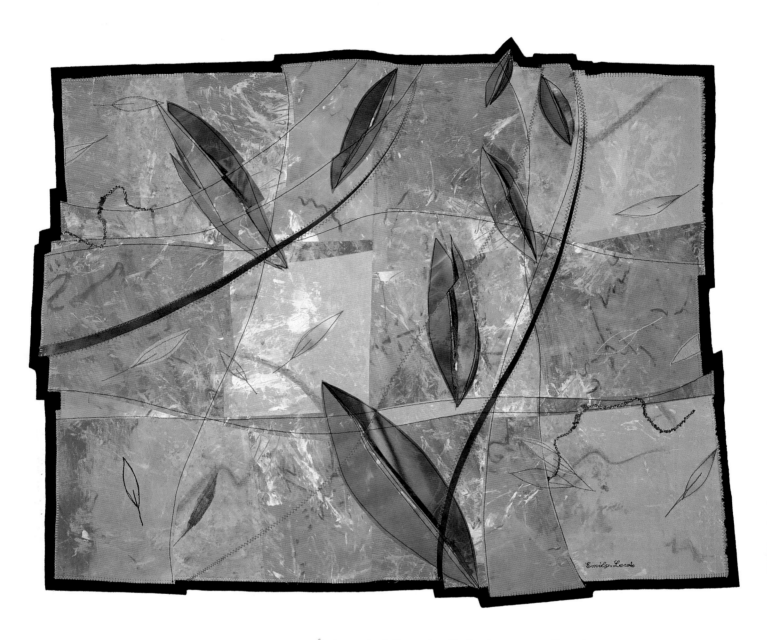

Emily K. Lewis
Cincinnati, Ohio

Georgian Spring
Pima cotton, acrylic paint, fabric
paint, dye sticks, thread; fused,
collaged, embellished, machine
quilted and embroidered;
30 x 25 inches (76 x 64 cm)

I created *Georgian Spring* to express the change of seasons in the south which occurs over a brief period of time. The leaves on the live oak trees fall during a span of only a week or two and are replaced with new ones immediately. The trees in the south don't experience the long dormant winter of a northern United States climate. This leaf fall often occurs in warm weather, and it creates a flurry of leaves everywhere, a wonderful choreography in the air.

Katherine K. Allen

Ft. Lauderdale, Florida

Nocturne

Cotton duck, ink; mono-
printed, printed, machine
appliquéd and quilted;
51 x 49 inches (130 x 124 cm)

Gesture, movement, and color are the focus of my work. I try to preserve and highlight the beautiful, physical logic of nature that is embedded in the accidental. Rapidly and without too much advance planning, I work the fabric's surface using multiple layers of a monoprinting, silkscreening process I developed specifically for this series. Stitched lines are added to accentuate and clarify the serendipitous rhythms that develop during the printing.

Marilyn Easter Fashbaugh

Waldport, Oregon

Another Beautiful Day in Paradise

Cotton, sheer polyester, silk (some shared
hand dyed); fused, machine quilted; 36 x 20
inches (91 x 51 cm)

Last summer we had little rain on the Oregon Coast, resulting in many glorious days. But we need rain; we long for rain. So—here comes a cloud!

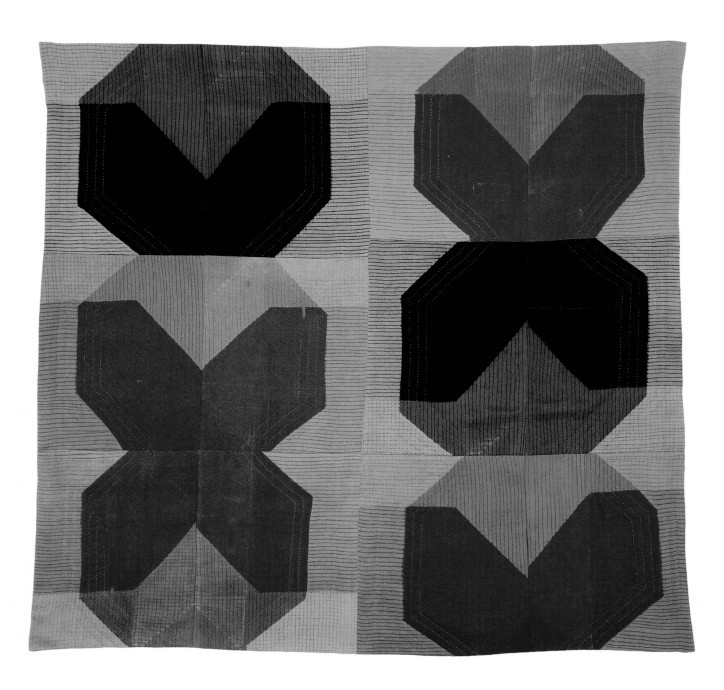

Ana Lisa Hedstrom

La Honda, California

Octet I

Silk piqué, cotton flannel, silk noil; resist dyed, discharge dyed, over dyed, machine pieced, hand quilted; 38 x 38 inches (97 x 97 cm)

I often find a musical metaphor in my work. I hope the viewer will respond to the color tones, the movement and repeats, and the rhythm within the geometric structure. I have been working with shibori techniques for over 25 years. It is a challenge to discover new ways to manipulate fabric and to create depth and unexpected color with the use of dye and dye remover. My goal is to be engaged with the process itself—having the material make music while I work.

Anne McKenzie Nickolson

Indianapolis, Indiana

A Question of Balance

Cotton broadcloth; machine pieced,
hand appliquéd and quilted;
47 x 47 inches (119 x 119 cm)

A Question of Balance is part of a body of work inspired by northern Renaissance paintings. What I most admire in these paintings is the artists' representation of textiles. I enjoy returning the images of cloth to a fabric composition.

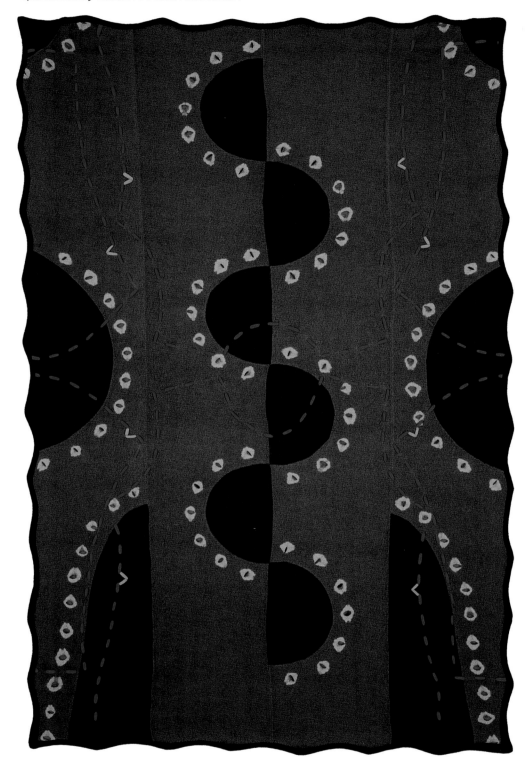

Jean Williams Cacicedo

Berkeley, California

Markers: Style 2-504

Wool, interfacing, linen; felted, slashed,
resist dyed, pieced, hand quilted;
37 x 56 inches (94 x 142 cm)

This work is an actual pieced cloth that is usually cut out and used to create a garment. This time, however, I left it whole but made reference to the garment with the stitch lines.

Jane A. Sassaman

Chicago, Illinois

Forgotten Garden

Hand-dyed, commercial cotton (designed by
the artist); machine appliquéd and quilted;
30 x 52 inches (76 x 132 cm)

This neglected garden has been invaded
by wild and undisciplined brambles. But,
there is still evidence of the formal and
cultivated blossoms beneath—optimism
in spite of adversity.

Ingrid Taylor

Fairbanks, Alaska

Resurrections

Cotton; machine pieced and
hand embroidered; hand and
machine quilted; 40 x 40
inches (102 x 102 cm)

I use basic blocks and fabrics (often called horrid or boring by friends) to give the traditional craft a dynamic and vibrant look. My approach is experimental, and perhaps symbolic. In this case, the crosses we bear, if transformed, lead to a meaningful whole.

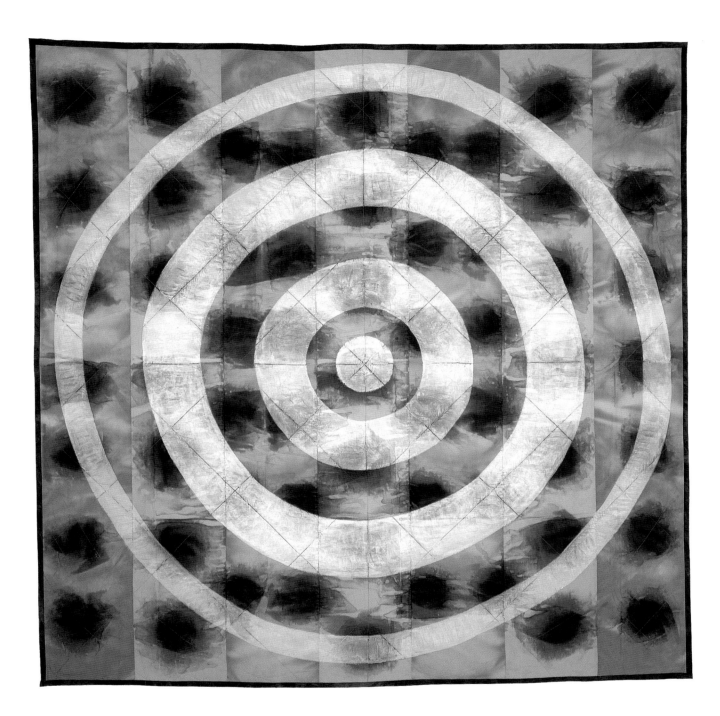

Mary Anne Jordan
Lawrence, Kansas

Target with Blue Stains
Hand-dyed cotton, indigo stains;
machine pieced and quilted;
72 x 72 inches (183 x 183 cm)

I am interested in the marks, the stains, and the drips that occur in our daily lives. These marks are often accidental—the aspects of our lives that cannot be controlled. The marks also become evidence of our own humanity. Because of our effort to keep appearances clean, straight, and tidy, each drip or stain is a defiant revelation.

Nancy Gipple

Afton, Minnesota

Wild Flowers

Assorted fabrics, raffia, ribbon,
string, crocheted fragments,
fishing seine, netting, thread;
collaged, sewn;
71 x 43 inches (180 x 107 cm)

Living in a time of a disposable
and throw-away culture, with its
wastefulness, carelessness, and
alienation, I find myself taking
refuge in the quilt with its tradition
of caring and frugality—to reuse,
recycle, remember, re-examine,
and reconnect.

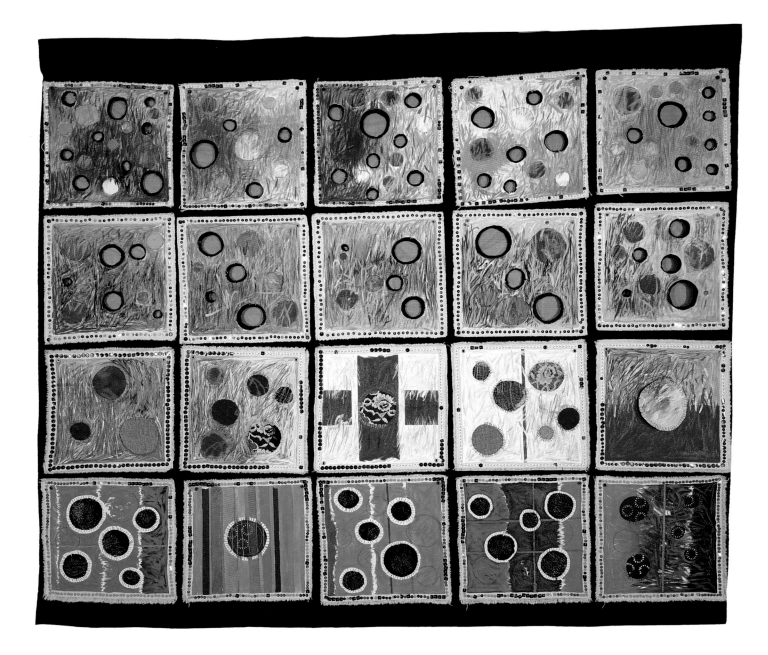

Janet Lipkin

Richmond, California

In Search of Nothing

Canvas, acrylic paint, sequins,
thread, netting, lace; hand
pieced and appliquéd, hand
embroidered and quilted;
52 x 45 inches (132 x 114 cm)

This quilt was a journey into myself, looking for peace in a frightening universe, melting one color into the next. The holes represent what we do not know. On this inward journey, I was thinking deeply about myself and the world around me, without exploring specific events.

Chiaki Dosho

Kawasaki-shi,
Kanagawa-ken, Japan

Bubble II

Old Japanese silk kimono fabric,
wool, cotton, synthetic fiber;
machine pieced and embroidered,
hand and machine quilted;
69 x 84 inches (175 x 213 cm)

People are like bubbles; in the end, they disappear. For this piece, I wanted to efficiently use as much of the cloth as I could without cutting it into small pieces, so that it would retain its charm. I see the creative influence of the fabric designer as being represented in this piece as well as myself.

Cosabeth Parriaud

Levallois, France

Rayures et Transparences I

Commercial cotton and synthetic
fabric hand painted by the artist;
machine appliquéd and quilted;
32 x 32 inches (81 x 81 cm)

This quilt concentrates on three directions that I have been following for a few years—painting fabrics, using stripes, and creating the effect of transparency. The manipulation of contrasting and cheerful fabrics is a continuous theme in my work; so is playing with simple shapes like squares, rectangles, and lines that escape from a too-geometric frame. While working, I attempt to eliminate what seems unnecessary and try to remember the wise and essential, guiding principle—less is more.

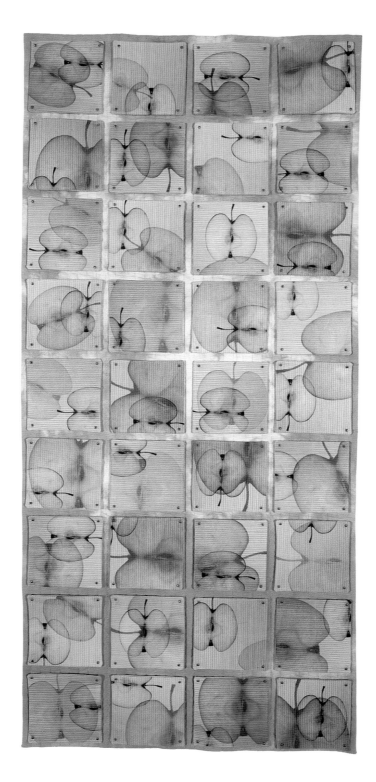

Julie Hirota

Roseville, California

Eden

Cotton canvas, metal brads;
photo transfer, hand dyed, quilted;
22 x 49 inches (56 x 124 cm)

Eden is a genesis for me, and a true departure from my original work. Tempted and intrigued by the possibility of combining traditional photography with digital photo manipulation in fiber, I photographed and superimposed an apple over a bamboo mat. This apple in Eden is my evolution.

Mary Ruth Smith

Waco, Texas

Obscurity

Sheer cotton, synthetic fabrics,
embroidery thread; machine
sewn, hand stitched and quilted;
29 x 42 inches (74 x 107 cm)

First, I was inspired by the fabrics. They spoke to me as I moved through cloth stores. Their sheerness, their structural and applied designs, their simple patterning—all caught my eye. I envisioned overlaying them and using an abundance of hand stitching to trace and reveal the images within a sandwich of fabrics. The pieced construction was inspired by *pojagi* wrapping cloths made by Korean women during the Choson Dynasty.

Anne Smith
Warrington, Cheshire, United Kingdom

Hopscotch
Recycled cotton fabric;
machine pieced, appliquéd and
embroidered, hand quilted;
57 x 53 inches (145 x 135 cm)

Hopscotch is a kids' game where you roll a stone and hop over chalked squares on a playground. What age would you be if you didn't know what age you are?

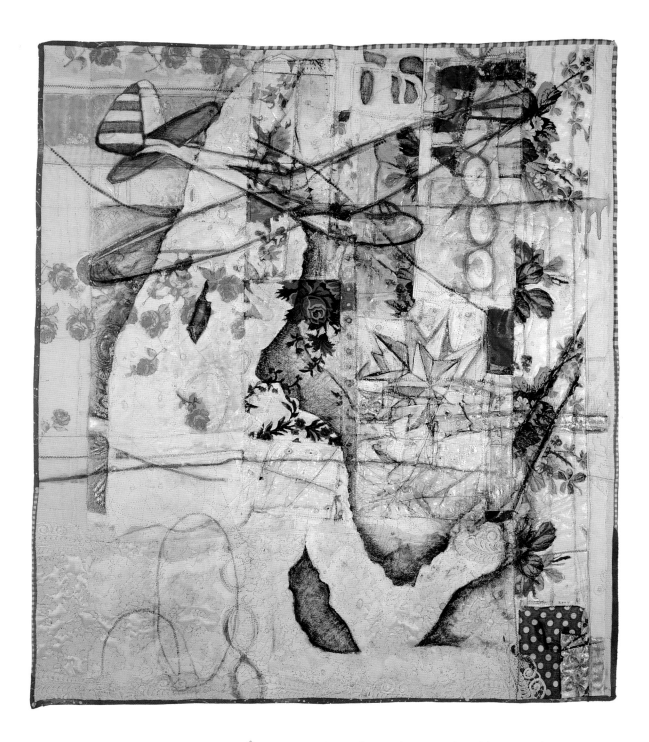

Jen Swearington
Asheville, North Carolina

Season of the Shark
Bed sheets, wedding gown, gesso,
shellac, charcoal, ink; pieced,
free-motion machine quilted;
35 x 41 inches (89 x 104 cm)

I created this quilt in February, when blues are the darkest. It is titled for a song that I listened to over and over again during many chilly, gray days. "...Something go wrong / Sink so low you even blame the sun / You blame it as the cause / Of the shadows on the wall..." I climbed in the window and traced a moment in time—my own winter shadow quietly waiting for the spring thaw. (Lyrics from "Season of the Shark," by Yo La Tengo)

Anna Torma

Baie Verte, New Brunswick, Canada

Rainy Day I

Found embroidered fabric, pieced textiles; hand embroidered and hand stitched, hand quilted; 52 x 57 inches (132 x 145 cm)

I feel I am a storyteller, using my private diary pages with drawings, text, and paintings from both my early experiences in Hungary and my recent life in Canada

Award for Best of Show

Susan Shie

Wooster, Ohio

Peace Mama Pie

Cotton, fabric paint, embroidery floss, thread, bead; painted, air and hand brushed, embellished, hand quilted; 22 x 42 inches (56 x 107 cm)

Peace Mama Pie is the latest in my body of quilted paintings that merge home, family, and kitchen with world politics and ethics, bringing a bully pulpit for world peace into our comfort zone, because we can't have comfort when we lose peace. We tend to deny the world's chaos when we sit in the safety of our private homes. Peace is lost in the world now, and women must demand its return and safekeeping.

Bonnie Peterson

Elmhurst, Illinois

Upper Peninsula

Heat transfers of maps and photographs, silk, velvet, brocade, sheer fabric; printed, hand and machine stitched, painted, embroidered; 48 x 50 inches (122 x 127 cm)

Many of my explorations and adventures in the wilds of the Upper Peninsula of Michigan are recounted with embroidered maps, stories and photographs. One backcountry ski trip to the top of Mt. Houghton is recounted with embroidery in the border. At the end of this trip, I photographed a snowbound truck at the base of the mountain and stacks of logs waiting to be shoveled out in the spring.

Angela Moll
Santa Barbara, California

Secret Diary 15: What Are You Doing?
Cotton silkscreened by the artist; machine pieced and quilted; 60 x 39 inches (152 x 99 cm)

I am looking into the intimate space where journals are written, where quilts are stitched. My "Secret Diaries" are journal entries screen-printed on fabric. The collaged and stitched diary fragments speak about intimacy and communication, as well as privacy and isolation. The oversized text is an invitation to read. Yet the stitched diaries are unreadable, revealing just the out-line of a life story—rhythm, pattern, layers. It is an open book, but a "Secret Diary."

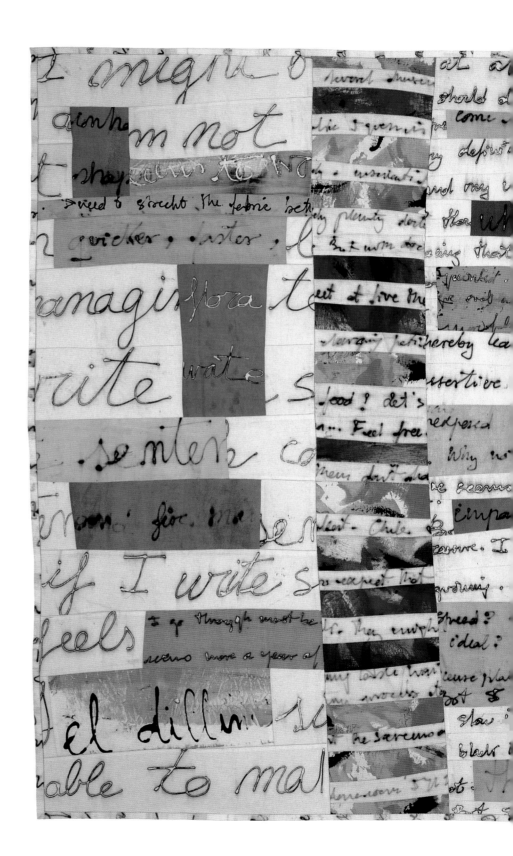

his is nor
it feels lo
are you doing?
single com
if I write

Tafi Brown

Alstead, New Hampshire

Jizo

Pieced cyanotype photographs on cloth, fabric hand dyed by artist, also Lunn/Mrowka hand-dyed fabric; machine pieced and quilted; 45 x 46 inches (114 x 117 cm)

Jizo is in response to time spent in Japan under a Fulbright Memorial Fellowship. It is also in response to over fourteen years of teaching art in public elementary schools. Emotionally and physically exhausted myself, I see neediness, anxieties, and indeed, anger increase seemingly exponentially among the children I teach.

Robin Schwalb

Brooklyn, New York

Beijing

Cotton, cotton-blend fabric; stenciled, direct and reverse-hand appliquéd, machine pieced, hand quilted; 85 x 77 inches (216 x 196 cm)

This quilt combines details of photographs and souvenirs from a trip to Beijing in December 2001. Most of the details are from the *hutongs* of Beijing—traditional alleyway neighborhoods—which are being razed in favor of modern chrome and glass behemoths. The color and humor of the finished piece reflect the happiness felt in the company of dear friends.

Katherine Knauer

New York, New York

Flying Goose

Commercial fabric,
fabric hand printed by the
artist; machine pieced and
appliquéd, hand quilted;
86 x 86 inches (218 x 218 cm)

All of my quilts combine traditional quilting patterns and techniques with a theme of current events. The seminal inspiration for this piece came in 1993 when Theresa Barkley gave me six yards of a hot-pink, smiley-condom cotton fabric, and the topic in the news was Safe Sex. (Other fabric contributors to this quilt were Woody Shimko, Paula Nadelstern, Robin Schwalb, Diane Schneck, and Jeanne Lyons Butler. I thank them for their encouragement and the persistent peer pressure that it took for me to finish this work in 10 years' time.)

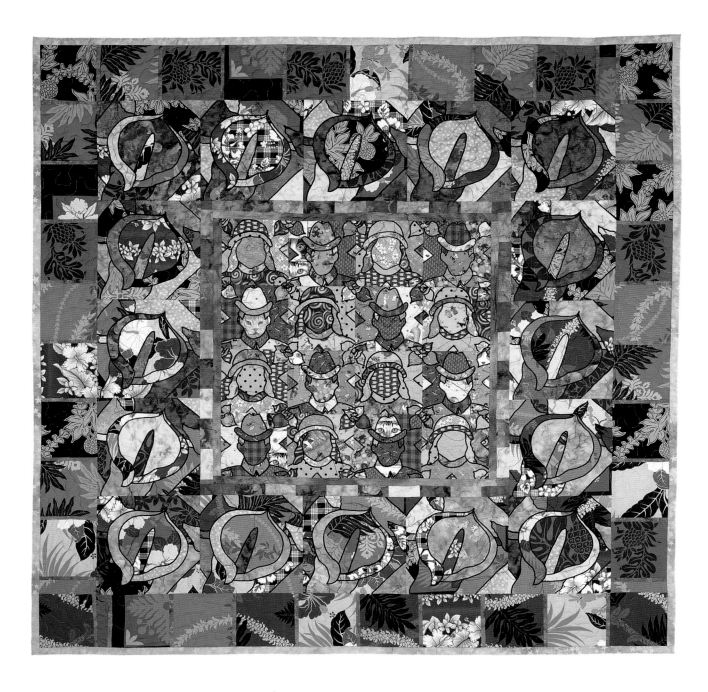

Therese May

San Jose, California

Alice and Don

Cotton and cotton-poly
blend fabrics; machine
appliquéd and quilted; 70 x
70 inches (178 x 178 cm)

Alice and Don were my parents. This quilt expresses
my gratitude to them for giving me life and my for-
giveness of them for giving me problems to work
through! In their portraits I used fabrics that reminded
me of happy children. In the calla lily border I used
Hawaiian fabrics, reminding me of relaxing warm
love. I calculated the size of the quilt at 70 x 70
inches, reminding me of Jesus teaching us to forgive
"seventy times seven."

Bean Gilsdorf
Portland, Oregon

Vacationland

Cotton; dyed, monoprinted,
relief printed, painted, machine
pieced, appliquéd, and quilted,
56 x 40 inches (142 x 102 cm)

Wendy Huhn

Dexter, Oregon

The Conversation

Painted canvas, transfers, stencils, beads; hand embroidered, screenprinted, machine quilted; 55 x 46 inches (140 x 117 cm)

Second in the series, the somnambulist continues on his journey.

Undecided if he is dreaming, or perhaps just a traveler in time.

He feels like he is awake.

Some of what he sees is familiar and comforting.

Other emotions are frightening, giving way to an uneasy feeling.

Like something is just not quite right.

Pam RuBert

Springfield, Missouri

PaMdora's Box

Commercial cotton, cotton hand
dyed by the artist, archival digital
prints, photo transfer, beads;
machine pieced, fused raw-edge
appliquéd, machine quilted;
71 x 43 inches (180 x 1109 cm)

This is my version of the myth of
Pandora with symbolic apples,
windows and worms. It's a crazy
world with plaid cats and polka dot
refrigerators. Hundreds of
machine-stitched webs cover my
house, and the colorful names of
viruses like MyDoom Sasser, and
Reeezak fill my laptop screen.
With the computer as the center
of this contemporary legend, what
kind of devilry has been released
into the world?! I can only watch
and wonder.

Linda MacDonald

Willits, California

Migration of the California Red-Legged Frog

Cotton broadcloth; airbrushed, hand painted, hand quilted; 36 x 39 inches (91 x 99 cm). On loan from the collection of Kathleen and Robert Kirkpatrick

A California wetlands consultant was caught moving red-legged frogs, an endangered species, out of the path of an East Bay housing development. The consultant had previously reported that no frogs were located on the site. Once the project was approved, he didn't feel that federal officials needed to be notified when red-legged frogs were found. He and his firm were found guilty in court and fined $70,000.

Andrea L. Stern

Chauncey, Ohio

Love Bird

Cotton, mica flakes; fused, appliquéd, machine and hand embroidered; 16 x 16 inches (41 x 41 cm)

This body of work represents a homecoming for me. Color, technique, and subject all take me back to the beginning, to the most basic of memories, the beloved home and art of my childhood.

Susan Else

Santa Cruz, California

Bingo!

Machine-sewn quilt sandwich covers an armature of plastic, foam, fiberfill, and wire; commercial and hand-dyed cotton, thread, cording, sculpey beads, paint, wire; 31 x 20 x 21 inches (79 x 50 x 53 cm)

During the past two years I have helped to run a weekly bingo game to raise money for our high school band. It's not your grandmother's bingo!

Jane Burch Cochran

Rabbit Hash, Kentucky

Deviled and Angel

Various fabrics, recycled articles (gloves, net blouse, handkerchief, doily), beads, buttons, sequins, paint, colored pencil, photocopies; machine pieced, hand embellished, hand appliquéd; 65 x 54 inches (165 x 137 cm)

This quilt contains two images I've used before but not together—the gloves forming wings, and the deviled egg plate (a Southern tradition). My muses were color and beautiful Thai silk. Although the title can be taken literally, *Deviled and Angel* became my 9/11 quilt since I was working on it 9/11/02, the one-year anniversary of that horrid day. The fortunes remind us of what might have been for the many lives that were taken that day.

Linda McCurry

Gilbert, Arizona

High-Fiber Quilt

Bread bags, foam rubber, acrylic paint, matte medium, wheat, bulghur wheat, raffia, straw placemats, thread, hand-discharged cotton binding; machine pieced, hand quilted with raffia; 26 x 32 inches (66 x 81 cm)

I love to laugh, and I love a good play on words. When a friend in my art quilt group made an off-hand remark about making a quilt without fabric, the idea for *High Fiber* came to mind. It was fun to take on the challenge of non-traditional materials.

Kim Ritter

Houston, Texas

Caution: Women at Work

Dye-paint serigraph and giclée print
on silk; machine pieced and quilted;
24 x 58 inches (61 x 147 cm)

This quilt is part of a new series called "Handy Women" that looks at the roles women are expected to fill in modern life. These quilts depict, tongue-in-cheek, the more practical side of womanhood, where my earlier quilts have explored the spiritual side of women. *Caution: Women at Work* is an ironic take on the changing face of gender roles in our society.

Amy Robertson
Cohasset, Massachusetts

Reservoir #5
Commercial batiks and hand-dyed
cotton; machine pieced and quilted;
37 x 55 inches (94 x 140 cm)

Feeling uprooted and disrupted by a move, but
now able to work in a studio with a view, I decided
to simplify and to pare down my work to the very
essence of the idea I wanted to communicate.
Through this process of abstraction, I found a way
to reveal more of myself.

Sandra LH Woock

Bethesda, Maryland

Pipedreams

Cotton; direct-application discharge, various resist techniques, including potato dextrin, over dyed, machine quilted; 38 x 59 inches (97 x150 cm)

Pipedreams, daydreams, misdirected musings; between reality and subconscious mind; or just impossible thought fleeing reality.

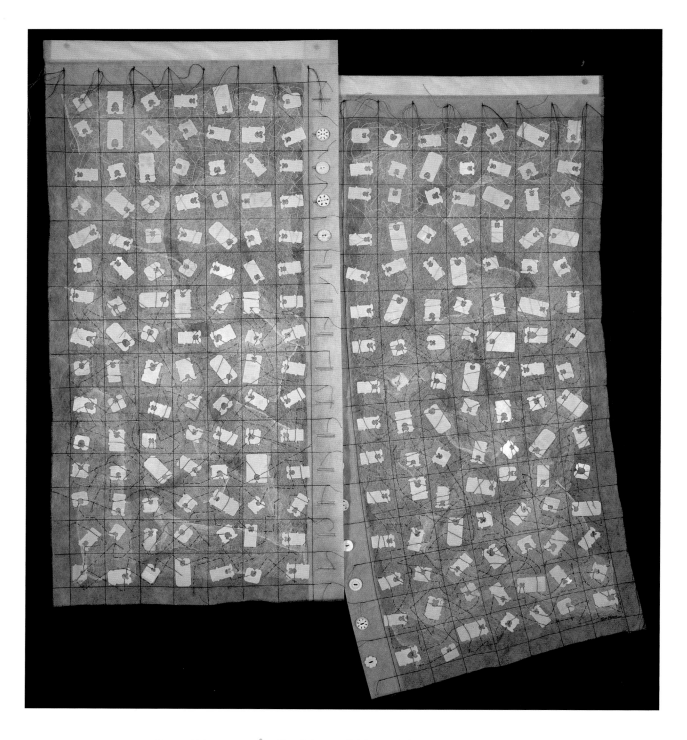

Sue Pierce

Rockville, Maryland

Seeking Closure

Non-woven synthetic fabric,
gossamer cheesecloth,
plastic bakery-bag closures,
vintage buttons; machine
and hand stitched;
35 x 39 inches (89 x 99 cm)

The intent of this work is to pose questions. The stitched grid is skewed; the sections do not connect neatly. Real life is never orderly. What went wrong? Will it be resolved? Translucent layers reveal opaque shapes that are related, yet evidence subtle variation. The forms are ghostlike reminders of their past life as fasteners. Freeform stitching anchors them in place, providing security—or restriction? The title says it all.

Daphne Taylor
New York, New York

Quilt Drawing #3
Silk, cotton embroidery
floss; machine pieced, hand
embroidered and quilted;
44 x 64 inches (112 x 163 cm)

In my recent work "Quilt Drawings," I utilize my painter's love of drawing. Lines reminiscent of landscape and figure are embroidered and composed on a grid that is then quilted, giving the viewer both geometric and organic movement. The interplay between the grid's rigid structure and the loose rhythm of life is simple, clear, and meditative.

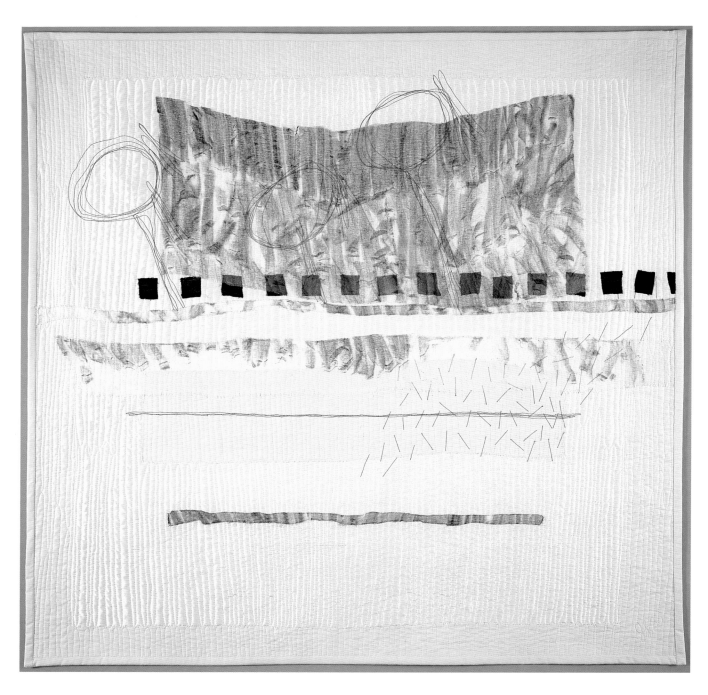

Jeanne Lyons Butler

Huntington, New York

White #28

Cotton, rayon, silk, cheesecloth, oil
paint, graphite, nylon thread;
appliquéd, machine quilted;
48 x 49 inches (122 x 124 cm)

Space and line converge in the layers of white. My
work in fiber combines earlier experience in painting
and drawing with the tactile nature of quilts. The work
draws its aesthetic strength from its restraint.
Sparseness as a compositional element conveys air
and infinity, and sometimes calmness, united with order
to absorb viewers into a sense of mystery. I yield to a
sense of quiet in my work.

Elizabeth Brimelow

Macclesfield, Cheshire,
United Kingdom

Fakenham Fen

Silk, cotton, blends, paper, nylon, beads,
sequins; hand and machine pieced, hand
appliquéd and embroidered, knotted;
65 x 77 inches (165 x 196 cm)

Landscape is where I live, what I look at, what I draw, and what I stitch. I love the flat open space of East Anglia. I am fascinated by marks made on the land, particularly those left by interventions such as planting, harvesting, and ploughing. I look for qualities in my observational drawings to bring to my textiles, and I work with cloth for its tactile qualities, its intimacy, and substance.

Clare Plug

Napier, New Zealand

To R.H. 2

Cotton fabric discharge dyed by the
artist; machine pieced and quilted;
70 x 55 inches (178 x 140 cm)

I made this work as a tribute to one
of my favorite New Zealand artists,
Ralph Hotere.

Patricia Mink

Johnson City, Tennessee

Wall Quilt #25

Linen, photograph of a wall
in Cordoba, Spain; inkjet
printed, dyed, machine
embroidered, quilted; 36 x
50 inches (191 x 127 cm)

This work is part of an ongoing series, exploring the complex surfaces of aging walls, using photographic imagery on fabric. The different patterns and textures that occur in the wall as a result of construction, deterioration, and reconstruction set up interesting visual relationships and contrasts when reproduced in softer materials.

Ardyth Davis

White Stone, Virginia

Sky Disc 1 / Green

Hand-painted silk, silk organza,
colored pencil, silver thread;
drawn, pleated, hand
appliquéd and quilted,
machine pieced and bound;
52 x 56 inches (132 x 142 cm)

Circular forms have been the focus of my recent work—usually sculptural fiber discs of pleated silk with crochet appliqué, but not usually on a rectangular ground. As I grow older, my thoughts often turn to the mysteries of existence—the universe, stars, and planets. Drawing the moon was an emotional experience for me.

Jo Ann Czekalski

Lexington, Kentucky

Untitled

Hand-dyed and ink-jet
printed silk, photograph;
machine pieced, hand
quilted, stiched shibori;
18 x 17 inches (46 x 43 cm)

I enjoy the process of manipulating fabric and dying it into patterns created by that manipulation—the Japanese art of shibori. I knew immediately, when I saw the light streaming through the window and creating an abstract pattern on the table and carpet, that I wanted to incorporate the image into a quilt and use stitched-resist shibori to recreate the radiating lines of light.

June O. Underwood

Portland, Oregon

Consider the Horse Chestnut

Silk charmeuse, cotton batting and backing,
computer-manipulated artist's photographs;
printed, over-painted, machine stitched;
51 x 39 inches (130 x 99 cm)

"Consider the lilies of the field, how they grow; they toil not, neither do they spin. Even Solomon in all his glory was not arrayed like one of these." The horse chestnut (*Aesculus hippocastanum*), like the lily, has little practical value but much shining beauty. Its season, like our own, is all too short. The technical processes of *Consider the Horse Chestnut* have theoretical ties to David Hockney's photographic experiments of the 1980s.

Elia Woods

Oklahoma City, Oklahoma

A Salad Ballad

Cotton, photo transfer;
machine pieced and quilted;
28 x 35 inches (71 x 89 cm)

Most of my imagery comes from my daily life—our gardens, neighbors and neighborhood. My current work is a series of photo quilts entitled "Vegetable Prayers," that celebrates the tremendous beauty and diversity of ordinary vegetables and the life of the gardens and soil in which they grow. I hope my work conveys a sense of the importance of community, the beauty of everyday life, and our relatedness with all of creation.

Nancy Whittington
Chapel Hill, North Carolina

Rippling Pond
Silk dupioni; resist dyed, hand painted, screenprinted, hand pieced and quilted; 98 x 66 inches (249 x168 cm)

A ripple expands on the still surface of a pond. The pond's stillness is the background in which the ripple occurs. Like positive and negative space, we experience one simultaneously with the other. In my work I am fascinated by what is clearly shown on the pictorial surface of the quilt and the mystery of what is implied, but unseen. The rippling movement swirls the water in full phase but how did it begin, how far will it travel, and what lies beneath?

Barbara J. Schneider

McHenry, Illinois

Reflections, Var. 7,
Brushy Creek, Kansas, MO

Hand-dyed cotton and rayon,
black-and-white shibori fabric by
Phil Jones; fused, machine quilted;
35 x 46 inches (89 x 117 cm)

This piece is part of a series based on photographs of moving water. The series explores the concept of reflection and how to capture the essence of images that are not physically there, images made of light and movement, images that are infinitely variable. It's also about what is beneath the surface that can be seen. And lastly, reflection is what I do throughout my work process, as well as what I hope viewers do as they look at the completed work.

Nelda Warkentin

Anchorage, Alaska

Palmaceae

Painted silk, hand-dyed and commercial cotton, canvas; fused, machine pieced and quilted; 60 x 40 inches (152 x 102 cm)

My work is about rhythm and pattern. Living in Alaska and extensive traveling provide me with a wide range of visual influences. The patterns created by the sunlight, colors, and the environment unique to each locale are the basis for my work. The layers of painted silk over a background image add depth and complexity to my work as the viewer can see through the surface to the colors underneath.

Jeanne Benson

Columbia, Maryland

Arrangement for Mixed Greens
with Edible Flowers and
Raspberry Vinaigrette

Cotton, linen, beads; direct-
machine appliquéd, hand
embroidered, machine quilted;
36 x 24 inches (91 x 61 cm)

This piece is one in a series of quilts about two things I love— reading recipes and making appliqués. I made the first one, *Ratatouille*, in 1995. I think of each quilt as a collection of ingredients, like the butterflies and leaves of childhood. Shape is the tool that interests me most, and the recipes allow me to work with a variety of shapes as I research ingredients, solve design and layout problems, and choose my techniques.

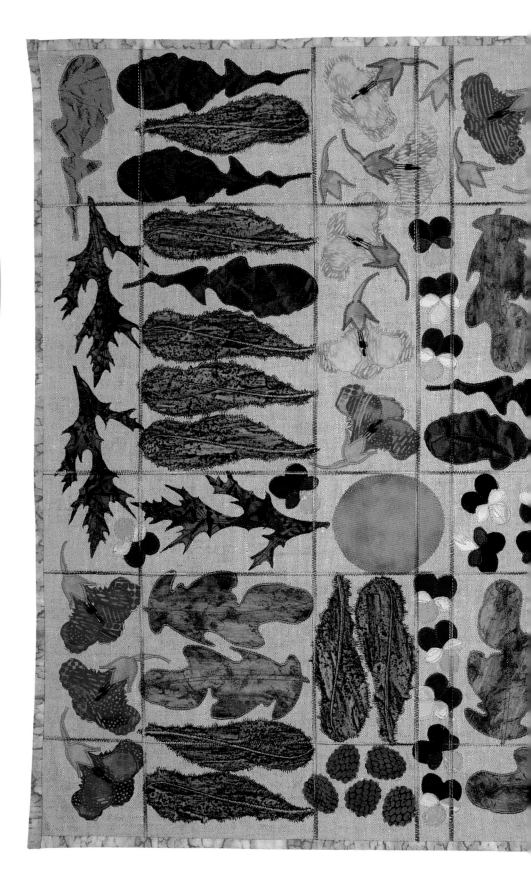

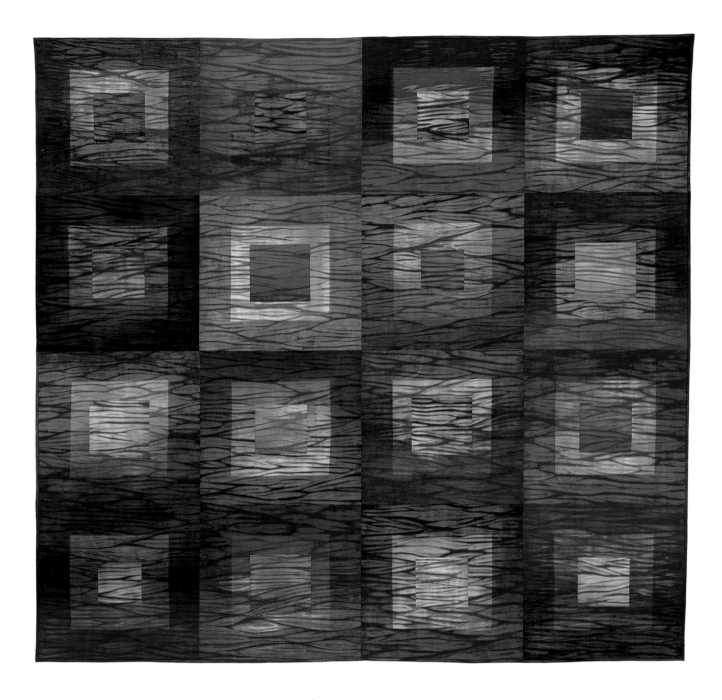

Jan Myers-Newbury

Pittsburgh, Pennsylvania

Homage to Albers

Kona cotton; dyed, clamp and
pole-wrap resist, dye under painted, machine pieced and quilted;
75 x 75 inches (191 x 191 cm)

In the 1950s and 1960s, colorist Josef Albers produced an extensive body of paintings titled "Homage to the Square." Each painting was distinct with regard to color placement within a set format—a square within a square within a square. A decade later, "Diamond-in-a Square" quilts, made by the Amish, graced the walls of the Whitney Museum— another example of uniqueness based on color choice. This quilt pays homage to both of these influences.

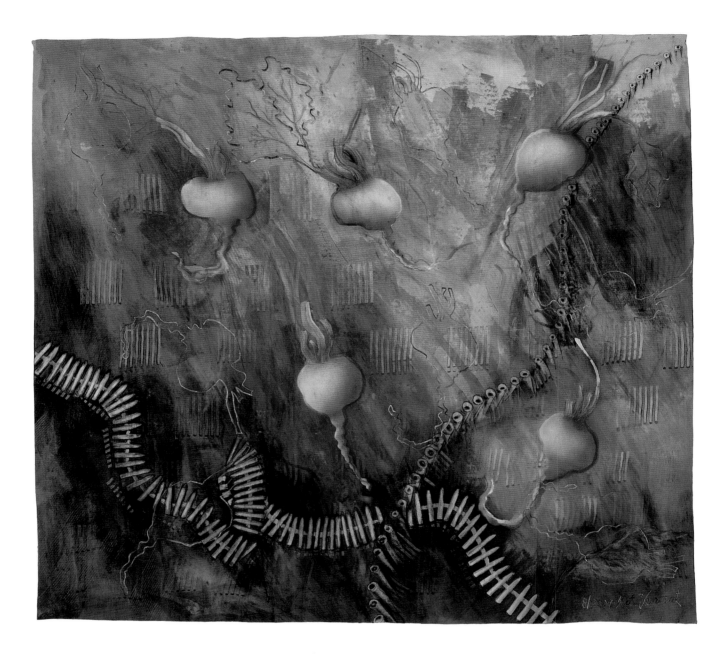

Kit Vincent
Ottawa, Ontario, Canada

Lancaster Series: Witness
Cotton canvas, acrylic paint,
pastels, textile paint; airbrushed,
machine embroidered and quilted;
60 x 54 inches (152 x 137 cm)

This quilt is about the brutal and shattering effects of war. My uncle was 22 and the bombardier on an RAF Lancaster when it was shot down over northern France in July of 1944. The pilot struggled to miss the town of Marcilly, and the plane crashed into a beet field with the loss of all aboard. Witnesses said it burned for 24 hours. The farmer who owns the field tells me that, even today, he still ploughs up fuselage and armaments from this site.

Joy Saville

Princeton, New Jersey

Les Fleurs de Babylone
Silk, cotton, linen; machine
pieced, constructed; 70 x 50
inches (178 x 127 cm)

Have you ever had your breath taken away by the color of dogwood trees, autumn leaves, or the view of the landscape as you drive over a hill? These are the frozen moments I strive to express in my work. Piecing cotton, linen, and silk fabrics in an impressionistic, painterly manner, I use the inherent quality of natural fabrics to absorb or reflect light, producing a constant interplay of light, texture, and color.

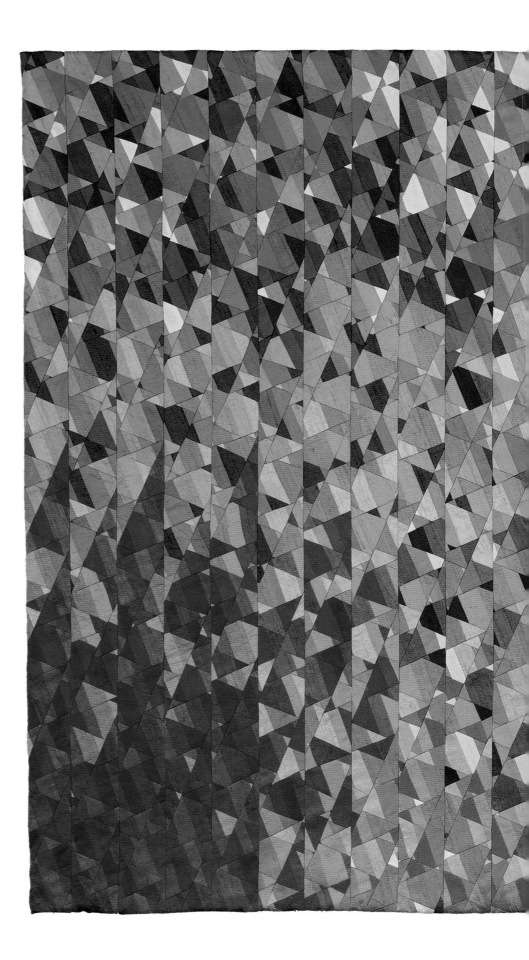

Sue Benner

Dallas, Texas

Fugue XI

Silk, cotton, recycled fabrics, dye, paint; fused, mono-printed, machine quilted; 51 x 31 inches (130 x 79 cm)

I began the "Fugue" series with thoughts of overlapping themes, creating complexity out of layered simplicity, and my love of this musical form—the fugue. I grew up in a Lutheran school and church, and the music of J. S. Bach has been an influence throughout my life. His music is beautiful, ordered, and sturdy.

Sylvia H. Einstein

Belmont, Massachusetts

Portal

Hand-dyed cotton and silk, commercial fabric, cotton blends, antique veil, antique yo-yos; pieced, appliquéd, machine embroidered and quilted; 33 x 33 inches (84 x 84 cm)

I made a collage with commercial and hand-dyed fabrics I had collected. I then added antique yo-yos, veiling, and machine-embroidered selected areas. Out of the dialogue with material and technique comes the finished quilt.

Beatriz Grayson

Winchester, Massachusetts

Stage Set

Un-sized and dye-painted
commercial and hand-dyed
cottons, ikats and batiks;
hand and machine pieced,
fused and hand quilted;
42 x 32 inches (107 x 82 cm)

The quilt medium is, for me, a metaphor for making the best of life, of the cards one is dealt. My work reflects notions of appreciating the chance encounter, embracing diversity, and tolerating the juxtaposition of seemingly unrelated textures. I like to think that I live the examined life and that I revise my choices for the best-quilted outcome.

Paula Nadelstern

Bronx, New York

Kaleidoscopic XXX:
Tree Grate, 53rd and 7th

Cotton, silk; machine
pieced, hand quilted;
59 x 52 inches (150 x 132 cm)

I aimed for an unsettling conceptual shift, taking a symmetrical object that New Yorkers usually ignore and always assume will be solid, and pulling the ground out from under it.

Lori Lupe Pelish

Niskayuna, New York

Safe in Suburbia
Commercial cotton; machine appliquéd, embroidered, and quilted; 69 x 41 inches (155 x 104 cm)

The comfortable and passive beauty of an American backyard represents a boundary that seduces and safely enfolds the creative spirit. But desires and yearnings are left unexplored until the artist discovers the way.

Deidre C. Adams
Littleton, Colorado

Passages
Commercial cotton, acrylic paint,
metallic thread; machine pieced,
appliquéd, and quilted, embellished;
19 x 27 inches (48 x 69 cm)

Life is a series of challenges, and priorities change as we get older. The way I view things now is very different from the way I did ten, twenty, or thirty years ago. *Passages* suggests progression along a journey and the things we encounter along the way that shape our views.

Deborah Herring

Dallas, Texas

Aunt Gracie in Stripes

Cotton; machine pieced and quilted.
Fabric sandwiches were quilted in parallel
rows 1 cm apart; panels were cut into 2½-
inch squares, with colors arranged in bars;
18 x 48 inches (46 x 122 cm)

I think most people see quilts as a nostalgic reminder of the past. If this quilt represents the family, its construction first represents the whole; then it's precisely cut apart and very deliberately put back together. Now pieced and quilted, it may look interesting, but it neither covers completely nor provides much warmth. How much harder must reconstructed families work?

Harumi Iida

Kamakura, Kanagawa, Japan

Step by Step

Commercial cotton, old *yukata* (Japanese summer kimono) cotton; hand and machine pieced, hand quilted; 47 x 47 inches (119 x 119 cm)

Whoever visits Hasedera Temple in Nara, Japan, needs to walk through a long corridor from the temple gates to the main temple complex. This corridor is a stairway with numerous twists and bends. Even if you stop along the way and look up, you cannot see your goal. You are forced to look at your feet and take it one step at a time, believing that you will eventually meet the Buddha.

Eleanor McCain

Shalimar, Florida

Crosses Study, Black/Yellow

Commercial and hand-dyed cotton;
machine pieced and quilted;
96 x 68 inches (244 x 173 cm)

Quilting is grounded in American history, family, community, and common experience. Art quilts are living documents of cultural history, expressing artistic, emotional, and spiritual values, particularly those of women. The traditional nine-patch block appeared in American patchwork quilts around 1800. Variations on this block over the subsequent 200 years seem to be infinite. The weight, balance, and visual impact of this pattern have fascinated me. *Crosses Study, Black/Yellow* is an investigation of color, contrast, and size relationships within the nine-patch form.

Lisa Call

Parker, Colorado

Structures #31

Cotton hand dyed by the artist;
machine pieced and quilted;
53 x 34 inches (135 x 86 cm)

I work in series that have an element or motif unifying the separate works in a collection. Look for one or more "E" shapes in the "Structures" quilts. The motif is more recognizable in some work than in others as the size, shape, and composition evolve over time. In *Structures #31,* the "E" has picked up an additional line with the individual units coming together to create movement across the surface of the work.

About the Dairy Barn

The Dairy Barn Southeastern Ohio Cultural Arts Center is a unique arts facility in the Appalachian foothills. Its year-round calendar of events features both juried and curated exhibitions of work by regional, national, and international artists. In addition, the facility is the venue for festivals, performances, and a full range of classes for children and adults.

The history of the Dairy Barn is as colorful as its exhibits. Built in 1913, the structure housed an active dairy herd until the late 1960s. After sitting idle about 10 years, the building was scheduled for demolition. Fortunately, local artist Harriet Anderson and her husband, Ora, recognized the building's potential as a much-needed regional arts center. They worked tirelessly to rally community support to save the dilapidated structure. With only nine days to spare, the demolition order was reversed, and the building was placed on the National Register of Historic Places. The Dairy Barn Southeastern Ohio Cultural Arts Center, a nonprofit organization, was born.

The architects retained the original character of the building through several renovation projects as it evolved from a seasonal, makeshift exhibit space into a first-class, fully accessible arts facility. Early 2001 saw the completion of a one million dollar renovation project. The ground level

now houses a 6,600-square-foot exhibition space and a 400-square-foot retail gift shop that features work by regional and exhibiting artists. The formerly unused 7,000-square-foot upper-level haymow now includes two large classroom spaces; three large multipurpose rooms suitable for classes, performances, and special events; offices for the staff; and storage space.

The Dairy Barn is supported by admissions, memberships, corporate sponsorships, grants, and donations. The staff is assisted by a large corps of volunteers who annually donate thousands of hours of time and talent. For a calendar of events and information about other Dairy Barn programs, contact the Dairy Barn Cultural Arts Center, P.O. Box 747, Athens, Ohio 45701, USA; phone, 740-592-4981; or visit the Internet at www.dairybarn.org.

Show Itinerary

The complete Quilt National '05 collection will be on display from May 28 through September 5, 2005 at the Dairy Barn Cultural Arts Center located at 8000 Dairy Lane in Athens, Ohio. Three separate groups of Quilt National '05 works (identified as Collections A, B, and C) will then begin a two-year tour to museums and galleries. Tentative dates and locations are listed below. It is recommended that you verify this information by contacting the specific host venue prior to visiting the site.

For an updated itinerary, including additional sites, or to receive information about hosting a Quilt National touring collection, contact the Dairy Barn Arts Center.

P.O. Box 747, Athens Ohio, 45701
Phone: 740-592-4981
E-mail: artsinfo@dairybarn.org
Internet sites: www.dairybarn.org; www.quiltnational.com

5/28 - 9/5/05	Athens, OH; Dairy Barn Cultural Arts Center
9/25 - 11/06/05	St. Charles, MO; The Foundry [A, B, and C]
12/2 - 1/15/06	Boone, NC; Turchin Center for the Visual Arts [B]
1/26 - 4/16/06	Columbus, OH; Riffe Gallery [C]
1/28 - 3/14/06	Sturgeon Bay, WI; Miller Art Museum [A]
4/6 - 4/9/06	Lancaster, PA; Quilters' Heritage Celebration [A and B]
6/3 - 9/3/06	Lowell, MA; American Textile History Museum [C]
7/1 - 8/31/06	Brigham City, UT; Brigham City Museum-Gallery [A]
10/7 - 12/2/06	Paducah, KY; Museum of the American Quilters Society [A and B]
11/2 - 11/5/06	Houston, TX; International Quilt Festival [C]
4/12 - 4/15/07	Lancaster, PA; Quilters' Heritage Celebration [C]
10/4 - 11/23/07	Laurel, MS; Lauren Rogers Museum of Art [C]

Artists' Index

Miriam Nathan-Roberts
Berkeley, California
Page 10

Anne McKenzie Nickolson
Indianapolis, Indiana
Page 39

Cosabeth Parriaud
Levallois,
France
Page 48

Lori Lupe Pelish
Niskayuna, New York
Pages 7, 98–99

Bonnie Peterson
Elmhurst, Illinois
Page 55

Mirjam Pet-Jacobs
Waalre,
The Netherlands
Page 16

Sue Pierce
Rockville, Maryland
Pages 6, 74

Clare Plug
Napier,
New Zealand
Page 78

Emily Richardson
Philadelphia, Pennsylvania
Pages 6, 19

Kim Ritter
Houston, Texas
Page 71

Amy Robertson
Cohasset, Massachusetts
Page 72

Pam RuBert
Springfield, Missouri
Pages 64–65

Dinah Sargeant
Newhall, California
Page 27

Jane A. Sassaman
Chicago, Illinois
Pages 41, contents page

Joy Saville
Princeton, New Jersey
Pages 92–93, contents page

Barbara J. Schneider
McHenry, Illinois
Pages 8, 86

Robin Schwalb
Brooklyn, New York
Page 59

Sandy Shelenberger
Conneaut, Ohio
Pages 12, 18

Susan Shie
Wooster, Ohio
Page 54

Anne Smith
Warrington, Cheshire,
United Kingdom
Pages 12, 51

Mary Ruth Smith
Waco, Texas
Page 50

Janet Steadman
Clinton, Washington
Pages 6, 14

Andrea Stern
Chauncey, Ohio
Page 67

Jen Swearington
Asheville, North Carolina
Page 52

Daphne Taylor
New York, New York
Page 75

Ingrid Taylor
Fairbanks, Alaska
Page 42

Anna Torma
Baie Verte, New Brunswick,
Canada
Page 7, 53

June O. Underwood
Portland, Oregon
Page 82

Kit Vincent
Ottawa, Ontario,
Canada
Page 91

Nelda Warkentin
Anchorage, Alaska
Page 87

Barbara W. Watler
Hollywood, Florida
Page 23

Nancy Whittington
Chapel Hill, North Carolina
Pages 84–85

Jeanne Williamson
Natick, Massachusetts
Page 13, cover

Sandra LH Woock
Bethesda, Maryland
Page 73

Elia Woods
Oklahoma City, Oklahoma
Page 83